THE WHOLESOME GARDEN

Written by Brittani Ramirez
Illustrations by Havilah G. Todd

WHO IS YAH?

In this story about clean and unclean foods, we will refer to God as **Yah**.
God is a title and not His actual Name.
It is like calling your father DAD, but he actually has a name.

God's Name in Hebrew is spelled with four letters:
Yod, Hey, Vav, Hey.
YHWH is the representation of these letters.
You pronounce His Name as Yahuah or for short, Yah.

We hope you enjoy this journey and find courage in Yah's love and guidance!

In the beautiful world Yah made so bright,
All plants and animals live in His light.

His loving wisdom, shining so clear,
Helps us know which way to stear.

"See here," they murmured, leafing through the Book,
"In Leviticus 11, let's take a closer look.

It shares wisdom on which foods to cook,
And which ones, for our well-being, we should overlook."

MENU

"The pig, the rabbit, and the camel too,
Though each has something special they do,

They don't chew the cud like clean animals do,
So Yah says they're unclean, for me and you."

"And in the waters, wide and blue,
Fish with fins and scales are good for you.

But shellfish and others, Yah says 'No,'
They're unclean, the Scriptures show."

"But why?" they pondered, their curiosity unfurled,
So, they invited wisdom, their questions to be twirled.

In prayer, they uncovered Yah's wisdom, like a pearl,
His laws protect and guide us in this world.

"Yah, in His wisdom," they said with delight,
"Made these laws to be just right.

They keep our bodies good and strong,
His love is shown through these rules all along."

From that day on, the children knew,
Yah's food rules were there to help them too.

They ate the foods that made them strong,
And kept their faith in Yah all along.

So, this story helps us see,
Yah's wisdom is where we should be.

By following His laws, we show our love,
And stay close to Him, like a hand in a glove.

This story reminds us, Yah's wisdom is true,
His laws and His love are meant for me and you.

When we follow His rules, we show Him we care,
And stay in His love, always and everywhere.

BIBLICALLY CLEAN

LAND ANIMALS
(DIVIDED HOOF AND CHEW THE CUD)

CATTLE (COWS, BULLS)
SHEEP
GOATS
DEER
GAZELLE
ANTELOPE
BISON

SEA CREATURES
(MUST HAVE FINS AND SCALES)

SALMON
TUNA
TROUT
MACKEREL
HERRING
COD
SARDINES
BASS

BIBLICALLY UNCLEAN

LAND ANIMALS
(DO NOT HAVE BOTH A DIVIDED HOOF AND CHEW THE CUD)

PIGS (SWINE)
RABBITS
CAMELS
HORSES
DOGS
CATS
BEARS

SEA CREATURES
(DO NOT HAVE BOTH FINS AND SCALES)

SHRIMP
LOBSTER
CRAB
CLAMS
OYSTERS
SQUID
OCTOPUS
SCALLOPS
EEL

SUPPORTING SCRIPTURES

These scriptures form the foundation of Yah's food laws as outlined in the Torah. They provide guidance on which animals are clean and suitable for consumption and which animals are considered unclean and should be avoided.

DEUTERONOMY 14:8

THE PROHIBITION AGAINST EATING PORK (SWINE) AND OTHER UNCLEAN ANIMALS.

DEUTERONOMY 14:3-21

THE REITERATION OF THE LAWS REGARDING CLEAN AND UNCLEAN ANIMALS.

DEUTERONOMY 14:21

THE INSTRUCTION TO NOT EAT ANYTHING THAT HAS DIED NATURALLY.

LEVITICUS 11:1-47

THE DETAILED INSTRUCTIONS ON CLEAN AND UNCLEAN ANIMALS FOR FOOD.

LEVITICUS 20:25

YAH DISTINGUISHES BETWEEN CLEAN AND UNCLEAN ANIMALS FOR HIS PEOPLE.

BENEFITS OF FOLLOWING YAHS FOOD LAWS

There are so many great reasons to follow Yah's food laws!
Here are some to think about, and see how they help us live happy, healthy lives!

HEALTHY AND STRONG

YAH'S FOOD LAWS HELP US STAY HEALTHY BY SHOWING US WHICH ANIMALS ARE GOOD FOR OUR BODIES. CLEAN ANIMALS, LIKE COWS AND FISH WITH FINS AND SCALES, ARE SAFER TO EAT AND BETTER FOR US.

OBEYING YAH

WHEN WE EAT THE FOODS YAH SAYS ARE CLEAN, WE ARE SHOWING LOVE AND RESPECT FOR HIM. IT'S A WAY TO FOLLOW HIS WORD AND LIVE AS HE WANTS US TO.

BEING SPECIAL (SET-APART)

YAH'S PEOPLE ARE CALLED TO BE DIFFERENT FROM OTHERS. BY FOLLOWING HIS RULES, WE LIVE IN A WAY THAT HONORS HIM AND HELPS US REMEMBER WE ARE SPECIAL TO YAH.

CLOSER TO YAH

BY EATING THE WAY YAH TELLS US TO, WE REMEMBER HIS LOVE FOR US EVERY DAY AND GROW CLOSER TO HIM!